YOUR KNOWLEDGE HAS VALUE

AF144798

- We will publish your bachelor's and master's thesis, essays and papers

- Your own eBook and book - sold worldwide in all relevant shops

- Earn money with each sale

Upload your text at www.GRIN.com and publish for free

David Machin

Main causes of the Thirty Years War

GRIN Verlag

Bibliografische Information der Deutschen Nationalbibliothek:

Die Deutsche Bibliothek verzeichnet diese Publikation in der Deutschen National-
bibliografie; detaillierte bibliografische Daten sind im Internet über http://dnb.d-
nb.de/ abrufbar.

Imprint:

Copyright © 2012 GRIN Verlag GmbH
Druck und Bindung: Books on Demand GmbH, Norderstedt Germany
ISBN: 978-3-656-56042-5

This book at GRIN:

http://www.grin.com/en/e-book/266157/main-causes-of-the-thirty-years-war

With reference to the situation in the empire, outline the chief causes of the Thirty Years War.

The religious and constitutional struggle of the Thirty Years War was one of the longest and most destructive conflicts in modern history. The period leading up to the war was characterised simultaneously by an extreme piety and increasing confessional divide in the empire, yet in its numerous theological, political and legal forms, the confessional conflict alone cannot be considered the sole cause of the conflagration. A myriad of structural factors led to the disabling and ultimately destructive breakdown of the Imperial constitution by 1618. Socio-economic considerations and various political factors are emphasised to varying degrees by historians from differing backgrounds and schools of thought. The historiographical debate identifies several potential groups to blame in causing the crisis, highlighting either the rivalry between the territorial princes for dominance in the Empire, or the continuous power struggle between the princes and the Emperor. The outbreak of war must also be seen within the political context of European power politics, as the Habsburgs and Bourbons struggled for supremacy on the continent, whilst the Protestants represented an increasingly powerful bloc in northern Europe, threatening the status quo of Habsburg peripheral empires. The precarious balance of power was maintained only by the antiquated structures of the Holy Roman Empire. Under severe internal and external strain, it merely required a final spark, which it found in Bohemia.

Long-term causes of the war may be ascribed to the growing social, economic and religious instability during the sixteenth century. In this period, Germany enjoyed relative stability, whilst neighbouring France was beleaguered by the war of religion from 1562 to 1598. Yet Hughes argues this façade of stability is deceptive, pointing out its proximity to the Thirty Years War.[1] It is sometimes argued this was a period of German economic decline, which may have exacerbated religious tensions, however it was merely a period of economic change, as cities began to experience decline and trade shifted away from the Hanseatic league.[2] Nevertheless, there was a definite increase in pauperism and vagabondage in the years running up to 1618, as well as a sharp increase in criminality

---

[1] Michael Hughes, *Early Modern Germany, 1477 – 1806* (Philadelphia: University of Pennsylvania Press, 1992), p. 61

[2] Ibid, p. 11

between 1560 and 1600, demonstrated by the growth of robber gangs.[3] Ultimately, the wave of peasant revolts between the 1580s and 1620s was indicative of deep social and political tensions, which Hughes argues could be exploited for political ends, as religious tension coincided with the revival of social problems. [4]

By the outbreak of war in 1618, the Holy Roman Empire seemed anachronistic and antiquated. Fragmented and disjointed, it was comprised of almost a thousand separate and fissiparous, semi-autonomous principalities. Asch points out the absurdity of a *de iure* bi-confessional but *de facto* tri-confessional empire headed by an absolutist Catholic Emperor.[5] Religious uniformity under Catholicism secured the Emperor's position, but its erosion over the sixteenth century polarised the constituent parts of the empire and thus fuelled rivalry between its competing interests.

The emergence of Protestantism signified a real threat to Habsburg dominance of the imperial title and led to increasingly aggressive anti-Protestant policies. Wedgwood argues a common faith was the only binding force in the decaying empire.[6] Whilst the Religious Peace of Augsburg (1555) seemingly defused tensions better than in neighbouring France, Asch argues it left many questions unanswered and merely postponed a ticking time bomb of conflicts for the next generation.[7] Wedgwood asserts that whilst the principle of *cuius regio eius religio* maintained religious homogeneity for the individual states, it destroyed it for the empire.[8] Religious unity could not be simply confined to the level of domestic territorial affairs and hence it unwittingly accelerated the desire of some rulers for increased sovereign power. Moreover, the *reservatum ecclesiasticum,* a clause which forced Prince-bishops to relinquish their princely dignity if they converted to Protestantism, catalysed Protestant discontent with the pro-Catholic bias of the Emperor. As it was implemented by imperial decree, not a vote of the Imperial Diet, it was particularly controversial.[9] Arndt asserts that the 'geistliche Vorbehalt' would precipitate further

---

[3] Ibid, p. 76
[4] Ibid
[5] Ronald Asch, *The Thirty Years War: The Holy Roman Empire and Europe, 1618 – 48* (Basingstoke: Palgrave, 1997), p. 17
[6] C. V. Wedgwood, *The Thirty Years War* (Middlesex: Pelican Books, 1957), p. 42
[7] Asch, *The Thirty Years War,* p. 10
[8] Wedgwood, *The Thirty Years War,* p. 42
[9] Ed. Geoffrey Parker, *The Thirty Years War* (London: Routledge, 1997), p. 17

conflict as many bishoprics were secularised nevertheless.[10] Demonstrably, war was only narrowly avoided when the Archbishop Elector of Cologne converted to Lutheranism, in order to marry, and was hence deposed in 1583 and replaced by Ernest von Wittelsbach, increasing tensions further between Catholics and Protestants.[11]

The existence of Calvinism in the empire had serious political and confessional implications. Denied acceptance by the *Confessio Augusta* in 1530 and forbidden by the treaty of Augsburg, it eroded the middle ground between reformed Protestantism and Catholicism and by implication, acceptance of the political status quo. At the time of Augsburg, it was not uncommon for Protestant councillors to serve Catholic princes, yet a gradual polarisation of the three confessions entrenched attitudes and fixed mentalities as part of a broader process of *Konfessionalisierung*.[12] Asch argues that whilst confessional diversity may not have led to war alone, it was intertwined with political conflict.[13] The comparative isolation of Calvinists fuelled increasing political activism leading up to 1618, as they sought allies in the Netherlands, England and the French Huguenots. The conversion of the Elector of Brandenburg in 1613 to Calvinism meant two electors were Calvinists, which threatened the power base of the Habsburgs and thus increased tensions further.[14]

The religious struggle was inseparably bound to the power struggle between the Emperor and the nobility. Catholics stressed the personal authority of the Emperor, whom they knew would protect Catholicism, whilst Lutherans, though committed to the institutions of the Empire, tended to distinguish between the Emperor as an individual and as the *maiestas* of the Empire as a body politic.[15] After increasing violations of the Peace of Augsburg, Calvinists and more radical Lutherans took matters into their own hands. In 1608 the incident of Donauwörth epitomised a monarchical violation, as Rudolf was seen as intervening in a domestic Swabian affair, under the authority of the Lutheran Duke of Württemberg, in order to restore Catholicism in a mainly Protestant city. As a consequence, many generally conformist Lutherans were driven to the Palatinate camp, as many

---

[10] Johannes Arndt, *Der Dreißigjährige Krieg* (Stuttgart:Reclam, 2009), p. 31
[11] Hughes, *Early Modern Germany*, p. 70
[12] Asch, *The Thirty Years War*, pp. 16-17
[13] Ibid
[14] Asch, *The Thirty Years War*, p. 15
[15] Ibid, pp. 18-20

Protestants walked out of the Reichstag on the 27th April 1608.[16] Moreover, eleven days later the Protestant Union was formed, representing a significant elevation of tension from rhetoric to military alliances.

Yet, whilst *prima facie* interpretations of the confessional struggle may suggest the tensions leading to war were motivated by religious conviction, certain historical agents may have manipulated the situation to suit their own secular interests. Asch argues a primarily structural approach is insufficient in comprehending the political decisions made leading up to the war.[17] Pursuing a radical confessional policy in the years running up to 1618 became advantageous for princes dissatisfied with the status quo within the Empire and the relative position it afforded them.[18] Ultimately, Asch argues, the formation of the League and Union must be regarded as 'quite traditional dynastic' politics.[19]

Utilising this framework, the actions of various princes can be interpreted in the light of power politics, whose actions led to the fratricidal war. As the most powerful Calvinist in the Empire, Frederick V stood to gain considerable influence as head of a confessional alliance determined to counter Habsburg supremacy. Yet, on the other hand, Frederick truly was motivated by his religious convictions, purportedly accepting the Bohemian crown because of a 'divine calling' he felt he must obey.[20] Religion may have been an important factor for Frederick, who stood to lose his hereditary lands and electoral title in challenging the most powerful dynasty in Europe. However, Christian von Anhalt was highly influential as Frederick's Chancellor, motivated by personal ambition to attack the weakness of Habsburg authority according to Parker.[21]

However, Parker's Great Man approach, singling out Anhalt and his political machinations as largely responsible for the outbreak of war is too monocausal and ignores the broader socio-economic and religio-political concerns that led to the war. Holborn argues the chief factor was the struggle between the estates and the monarchy against a combustible backdrop of ambitious foreign powers, weak German states and the Bohemian

---

[16] Hughes, *Early Modern Germany*, p. 78
[17] Asch, *The Thirty Years War*, p. 7
[18] Ibid, p. 22
[19] Ibid
[20] Wedgwood, *The Thirty Years War*, p. 92
[21] Parker, *The Thirty Years War*, p. 34

crisis.[22] Indeed, the desire of the Habsburgs to wield absolute power can be considered a chief cause in the breakdown of the constitution that ultimately led to war.

The crippling of various supra-territorial organs of state and their unashamed pro-Catholic bias led most Protestants to lose faith in institutional security for their faith and lands, demonstrated as the Imperial Diet met only five times during Rudolph's reign (1576–1612).[23] Protestants felt the Emperor abused his office most blatantly in the Jülich-Cleves incident of 1610. Close to Westphalia and Cologne, it held strategic significance for Catholics. The Emperor was considered to have acted unfairly in sending troops. Consequently, the price of mediation was considered too high by many Protestants as the territory was divided under the Treaty of Xanten,[24] driving many Protestants towards external alliances, as in Bohemia.

Whilst the rights of Bohemian Protestants were safeguarded by the Letter of Majesty signed in July 1609, Ferdinand's regents implemented numerous provocative measures during the winter of 1617/18, establishing a censorship office and barring non-Catholics from civil offices.[25] Consequently, the Protestant nobility sought external allies, whom Parker argues they found in Anhalt and his network of powerful friends.[26] Many Protestants considered the Bohemian's plight to be emblematic of the wider threat the evangelical faith and German liberty faced. Frederick's support encouraged Bohemians to assert their right to practise their faith and depose Ferdinand on the 29th August 1619. This placed the Habsburg's monopoly of the Imperial title under threat, as Frederick's election made the Protestant electors a majority, even if the Saxon Elector remained a compliant Lutheran. The crisis seems to have been the final spark to a chain reaction of events that developed into the war.

However, a confessional 'tinder-box theory' is discredited by Hughes, who points out that Europe underwent a cooling in religious tension in the years running up to 1618 as the

---

[22] Hajo Holborn, *A History of Modern Germany: The Reformation* (Princeton: Princeton University Press, 1982), p. 305
[23] Hughes, *Early Modern Germany*, p, 71
[24] Parker, *The Thirty Years War*, p. 32
[25] Ibid, p. 39
[26] Ibid, p. 40

Spanish and the Dutch were treaty-bound to peace until 1621.[27] Holborn consolidates this view, arguing the confessional war began long after the enthusiasm for a religious war had lost a good deal of its original force.[28] In other words, internal and external top-down power struggles were intertwined with confessional conflict. The Bohemian crisis reflected trends seen elsewhere in the empire, but the armed camps had become so polarised that they were easily manipulated by the territorial princes and the Emperor.

In conclusion, the Thirty Years War was the product of a multitude of socio-economic and religio-political factors, manipulated by historical agents for their own secular ends. Whilst the conflict had implications for confessional identity, the real power movers utilised the religious question as a focal point for the dispute about imperial absolutism and the rivalries between the princes. Ultimately, without the power vacuum that had developed in the empire by the turn of the seventeenth century, the religious divide and harsh socio-economic conditions alone would not have been enough to trigger a confessional war of eschatological proportions.

---

[27] Hughes, *Early Modern Germany,* p. 79
[28] Holborn, *A History of Modern Germany,* p. 305

Bibliography:

Arndt, Johannes, *Der Dreißigjährige Krieg* (Stuttgart:Reclam, 2009)

Asch, Ronald, *The Thirty Years War: The Holy Roman Empire and Europe, 1618 – 48* (Basingstoke: Palgrave, 1997)

Holborn, Hajo, *A History of Modern Germany: The Reformation* (Princeton: Princeton University Press, 1982)

Hughes, Michael, *Early Modern Germany, 1477 – 1806* (Philadelphia: University of Pennsylvania Press, 1992)

Ed. Parker, Geoffrey, *The Thirty Years War* (London: Routledge, 1997)

Schmidt, Georg, *Der Dreißigjährige Krieg* (München: C.H.Beck, 1995)

Wegdwood, C. V, *The Thirty Years War* (Middlesex: Pelican Books, 1957)